Christ in Flanders

Honoré de Balzac

(Translator: Ellen Marriage)

Alpha Editions

This edition published in 2024

ISBN : 9789367245101

Design and Setting By
Alpha Editions
www.alphaedis.com
Email - info@alphaedis.com

As per information held with us this book is in Public Domain.
This book is a reproduction of an important historical work. Alpha Editions uses the best technology to reproduce historical work in the same manner it was first published to preserve its original nature. Any marks or number seen are left intentionally to preserve its true form.

CHRIST IN FLANDERS

At a dimly remote period in the history of Brabant, communication between the Island of Cadzand and the Flemish coast was kept up by a boat which carried passengers from one shore to the other. Middelburg, the chief town in the island, destined to become so famous in the annals of Protestantism, at that time only numbered some two or three hundred hearths; and the prosperous town of Ostend was an obscure haven, a straggling village where pirates dwelt in security among the fishermen and the few poor merchants who lived in the place.

But though the town of Ostend consisted altogether of some score of houses and three hundred cottages, huts or hovels built of the driftwood of wrecked vessels, it nevertheless rejoiced in the possession of a governor, a garrison, a forked gibbet, a convent, and a burgomaster, in short, in all the institutions of an advanced civilization.

Who reigned over Brabant and Flanders in those days? On this point tradition is mute. Let us confess at once that this tale savors strongly of the marvelous, the mysterious, and the vague; elements which Flemish narrators have infused into a story retailed so often to gatherings of workers on winter evenings, that the details vary widely in poetic merit and incongruity of detail. It has been told by every generation, handed down by grandames at the fireside, narrated night and day, and the chronicle has changed its complexion somewhat in every age. Like some great building that has suffered many modifications of successive generations of architects, some sombre weather-beaten pile, the delight of a poet, the story would drive the commentator and the industrious winnower of words, facts, and dates to despair. The narrator believes in it, as all superstitious minds in Flanders likewise believe; and is not a whit wiser nor more credulous than his audience. But as it would be impossible to make a harmony of all the different renderings, here are the outlines of the story; stripped, it may be, of its picturesque quaintness, but with all its bold disregard of historical truth, and its moral teachings approved by religion—a myth, the blossom of imaginative fancy; an allegory that the wise may interpret to suit themselves. To each his own pasturage, and the task of separating the tares from the wheat.

The boat that served to carry passengers from the Island of Cadzand to Ostend was upon the point of departure; but before the skipper loosed the chain that secured the shallop to the little jetty, where people embarked, he blew a horn several times, to warn late lingerers, this being his last journey that day. Night was falling. It was scarcely possible to see the coast of Flanders by the dying fires of the sunset, or to make out upon the hither shore any forms of belated passengers hurrying along the wall of the dykes that surrounded the open country, or among the tall reeds of the marshes. The boat was full.

"What are you waiting for? Let us put off!" they cried.

Just at that moment a man appeared a few paces from the jetty, to the surprise of the skipper, who had heard no sound of footsteps. The traveler seemed to have sprung up from the earth, like a peasant who had laid himself down on the ground to wait till the boat should start, and had slept till the sound of the horn awakened him. Was he a thief? or some one belonging to the custom-house or the police?

As soon as the man appeared on the jetty to which the boat was moored, seven persons who were standing in the stern of the shallop hastened to sit down on the benches, so as to leave no room for the newcomer. It was the swift and instinctive working of the aristocratic spirit, an impulse of exclusiveness that comes from the rich man's heart. Four of the seven personages belonged to the most aristocratic families in Flanders. First among them was a young knight with two beautiful greyhounds; his long hair flowed from beneath a jeweled cap; he clanked his gilded spurs, curled the ends of his moustache from time to time with a swaggering grace, and looked round disdainfully on the rest of the crew. A high-born damsel, with a falcon on her wrist, only spoke with her mother or with a churchman of high rank, who was evidently a relation. All these persons made a great deal of noise, and talked among themselves as though there were no one else in the boat; yet close beside them sat a man of great importance in the district, a stout burgher of Bruges, wrapped about with a vast cloak. His servant, armed to the teeth, had set down a couple of bags filled with gold at his side. Next to the burgher came a man of learning, a doctor of the University of Louvain, who was traveling with his clerk. This little group of folk, who looked contemptuously at each other, was separated from the passengers in the forward part of the boat by the bench of rowers.

The belated traveler glanced about him as he stepped on board, saw that there was no room for him in the stern, and went to the bows in quest of a seat. They were all poor people there. At first sight of the bareheaded man in the brown camlet coat and trunk-hose, and plain stiff linen collar, they noticed that he wore no ornaments, carried no cap nor bonnet in his hand, and had neither sword nor purse at his girdle, and one and all took him for a burgomaster sure of his authority, a worthy and kindly burgomaster like so many a Fleming of old times, whose homely features and characters have been immortalized by Flemish painters. The poorer passengers, therefore, received him with demonstrations of respect that provoked scornful tittering at the other end of the boat. An old soldier, inured to toil and hardship, gave up his place on the bench to the newcomer, and seated himself on the edge of the vessel, keeping his balance by planting his feet against one of those traverse beams, like the backbone of a fish, that hold the planks of a boat together. A young mother, who bore her baby in her arms, and seemed to belong to the working class in Ostend, moved aside to make room for the stranger. There was neither servility nor scorn in her manner of doing this; it was a simple sign of the goodwill by which the poor, who know by long experience the value of a service and the warmth that fellowship brings, give expression to the open-heartedness and the natural impulses of their souls; so artlessly do they reveal their good qualities and their defects. The stranger thanked her by a gesture full of gracious dignity, and took his place between the young mother and the old soldier. Immediately behind him sat a peasant and his son, a boy ten years of age. A beggar woman, old, wrinkled, and clad in rags, was crouching, with her almost empty wallet, on a great coil of rope that lay in the prow. One of the rowers, an old sailor, who had known her in the days of her beauty and prosperity, had let her come in "for the love of God," in the beautiful phrase that the common people use.

"Thank you kindly, Thomas," the old woman had said. "I will say two *Paters* and two *Aves* for you in my prayers to-night."

The skipper blew his horn for the last time, looked along the silent shore, flung off the chain, ran along the side of the boat, and took up his position at the helm. He looked at the sky, and as soon as they were out in the open sea, he shouted to the men: "Pull away, pull with all your might! The sea is smiling at a squall, the witch! I can feel the swell by the way the rudder works, and the storm in my wounds."

The nautical phrases, unintelligible to ears unused to the sound of the sea, seemed to put fresh energy into the oars; they kept time together, the rhythm of the movement was still even and steady, but quite unlike the previous manner of rowing; it was as if a cantering horse had broken into a gallop. The gay company seated in the stern amused themselves by watching the brawny arms, the tanned faces, and sparkling eyes of the rowers, the play of the tense muscles, the physical and mental forces that were being exerted to bring them for a trifling toll across the channel. So far from pitying the rowers' distress, they pointed out the men's faces to each other, and laughed at the grotesque expressions on the faces of the crew who were straining every muscle; but in the fore part of the boat the soldier, the peasant, and the old beggar woman watched the sailors with the sympathy naturally felt by toilers who live by the sweat of their brow and know the rough struggle, the strenuous excitement of effort. These folk, moreover, whose lives were spent in the open air, had all seen the warnings of danger in the sky, and their faces were grave. The young mother rocked her child, singing an old hymn of the Church for a lullaby.

"If we ever get there at all," the soldier remarked to the peasant, "it will be because the Almighty is bent on keeping us alive."

"Ah! He is the Master," said the old woman, "but I think it will be His good pleasure to take us to Himself. Just look at that light down there..." and she nodded her head as she spoke towards the sunset.

Streaks of fiery red glared from behind the masses of crimson-flushed brown cloud that seemed about to unloose a furious gale. There was a smothered murmur of the sea, a moaning sound that seemed to come from the depths, a low warning growl, such as a dog gives when he only means mischief as yet. After all, Ostend was not far away. Perhaps painting, like poetry, could not prolong the existence of the picture presented by sea and sky at that moment beyond the time of its actual duration. Art demands vehement contrasts, wherefore artists usually seek out Nature's most striking effects, doubtless because they despair of rendering the great and glorious charm of her daily moods; yet the human soul is often stirred as deeply by her calm as by her emotion, and by silence as by storm.

For a moment no one spoke on board the boat. Every one watched that sea and sky, either with some presentiment of danger, or because they felt the influence of the religious melancholy that takes possession of nearly all of us at the close of the day, the hour of prayer, when all nature is hushed save for the voices of the bells. The sea gleamed pale and wan, but its hues changed, and the surface took all the colors of steel. The sky was almost overspread with livid gray, but down in the west there were long narrow bars like streaks of blood; while lines of bright light in the eastern sky, sharp and clean as if drawn by the tip of a brush, were separated by folds of cloud, like the wrinkles on an old man's brow. The whole scene made a background of ashen grays and half-tints, in strong contrast to the bale-fires of the sunset. If written language might borrow of spoken language some of the bold figures of speech invented by the people, it might be said with the soldier that "the weather has been routed," or, as the peasant would say, "the sky glowered like an executioner." Suddenly a wind arose from the quarter of the sunset, and the skipper, who never took his eyes off the sea, saw the swell on the horizon line, and cried:

"Stop rowing!"

The sailors stopped immediately, and let their oars lie on the water.

"The skipper is right," said Thomas coolly. A great wave caught up the boat, carried it high on its crest, only to plunge it, as it were, into the trough of the sea that seemed to yawn for them. At this mighty upheaval, this sudden outbreak of the wrath of the sea, the company in the stern turned pale, and sent up a terrible cry.

"We are lost!"

"Oh, not yet!" said the skipper calmly.

As he spoke, the clouds immediately above their heads were torn asunder by the vehemence of the wind. The gray mass was rent and scattered east and west with ominous speed, a dim uncertain light from the rift in the sky fell full upon the boat, and the travelers beheld each other's faces. All of them, the noble and the wealthy, the sailors and the poor passengers alike, were amazed for a moment by the appearance of the last comer. His golden hair, parted upon his calm, serene forehead, fell in thick curls about his shoulders; and his face, sublime in its sweetness and radiant with divine love, stood out against the surrounding gloom. He had no contempt for death; he knew that he should not die. But if at the first the company in the stern forgot for a moment the implacable fury of the storm that threatened their lives, selfishness and their habits of life soon prevailed again.

"How lucky that stupid burgomaster is, not to see the risks we are all running! He is just like a dog, he will die without a struggle," said the doctor.

He had scarcely pronounced this highly judicious dictum when the storm unloosed all its legions. The wind blew from every quarter of the heavens, the boat span round like a top, and the sea broke in.

"Oh! my poor child! my poor child!... Who will save my baby?" the mother cried in a heart-rending voice.

"You yourself will save it," the stranger said.

The thrilling tones of that voice went to the young mother's heart and brought hope with them; she heard the gracious words through all the whistling of the wind and the shrieks of the passengers.

"Holy Virgin of Good Help, who art at Antwerp, I promise thee a thousand pounds of wax and a statue, if thou wilt rescue me from this!" cried the burgher, kneeling upon his bags of gold.

"The Virgin is no more at Antwerp than she is here," was the doctor's comment on this appeal.

"She is in heaven," said a voice that seemed to come from the sea.

"Who said that?"

"'Tis the devil!" exclaimed the servant. "He is scoffing at the Virgin of Antwerp."

"Let us have no more of your Holy Virgin at present," the skipper cried to the passengers. "Put your hands to the scoops and bail the water out of the boat.—And the rest of you," he went on, addressing the sailors, "pull with all your might! Now is the time; in the name of the devil who is leaving you in this world, be your own Providence! Every one knows that the channel is fearfully dangerous; I have been to and fro across it these thirty years. Am I facing a storm for the first time to-night?"

He stood at the helm, and looked, as before, at his boat and at the sea and sky in turn.

"The skipper always laughs at everything," muttered Thomas.

"Will God leave us to perish along with those wretched creatures?" asked the haughty damsel of the handsome cavalier.

"No, no, noble maiden.... Listen!" and he caught her by the waist and said in her ear, "I can swim, say nothing about it! I will hold you by your fair hair and bring you safely to the shore; but I can only save you."

The girl looked at her aged mother. The lady was on her knees entreating absolution of the Bishop, who did not heed her. In the beautiful eyes the knight read a vague feeling of filial piety, and spoke in a smothered voice.

"Submit yourself to the will of God. If it is His pleasure to take your mother to Himself, it will doubtless be for her happiness—in another world," he added, and his voice dropped still lower. "And for ours in this," he thought within himself.

The Dame of Rupelmonde was lady of seven fiefs beside the barony of Gavres.

The girl felt the longing for life in her heart, and for love that spoke through the handsome adventurer, a young miscreant who haunted churches in search of a prize, an heiress to marry, or ready money. The Bishop bestowed his benison on the waves, and bade them be calm; it was all that he could do. He thought of his concubine, and of the delicate feast with which she would welcome him; perhaps at that very moment she was bathing, perfuming herself, robing herself in velvet, fastening her necklace and her jeweled clasps; and the perverse Bishop, so far from thinking of the power of Holy Church, of his duty to comfort Christians and exhort them to trust in God, mingled worldly regrets and lover's sighs with the holy words of the breviary. By the dim light that shone on the pale faces of the company, it was possible to see their differing expressions as the boat was lifted high in air by a wave, to be cast back into the dark depths; the shallop quivered like a fragile leaf, the plaything of the north wind in the autumn; the hull creaked, it seemed ready to go to pieces. Fearful shrieks went up, followed by an awful silence.

There was a strange difference between the behavior of the folk in the bows and that of the rich or great people at the other end of the boat.

The young mother clasped her infant tightly to her breast every time that a great wave threatened to engulf the fragile vessel; but she clung to the hope that the stranger's words had set in her heart. Each time that the eyes turned to his face she drew fresh faith at the sight, the strong faith of a helpless woman, a mother's faith. She lived by that divine promise, the loving words from his lips; the simple creature waited trustingly for them to be fulfilled, and scarcely feared the danger any longer.

The soldier, holding fast to the vessel's side, never took his eyes off the strange visitor. He copied on his own rough and swarthy features the imperturbability of the other's face, applying to this task the whole strength of a will and intelligence but little corrupted in the course of a life of mechanical and passive obedience. So emulous was he of a calm and tranquil courage greater than his own, that at last, perhaps unconsciously, something of that mysterious nature passed into his own soul. His admiration became an instinctive zeal for this man, a boundless love for and belief in him, such a love as soldiers feel for their leader when he has the power of swaying other men, when the halo of victories surrounds him, and the magical fascination of genius is felt in all that he does. The poor outcast was murmuring to herself:

"Ah! miserable wretch that I am! Have I not suffered enough to expiate the sins of my youth? Ah! wretched woman, why did you lead the gay life of a frivolous Frenchwoman? why did you devour the goods of God with churchmen, the substance of the poor with extortioners and fleecers of the poor? Oh! I have sinned indeed!—Oh my God! my God! let me finish my time in hell here in this world of misery."

And again she cried, "Holy Virgin, Mother of God, have pity upon me!"

"Be comforted, mother. God is not a Lombard usurer. I may have killed people good and bad at random in my time, but I am not afraid of the resurrection."

"Ah! master Lancepesade, how happy those fair ladies are, to be so near to a bishop, a holy man! They will get absolution for their sins," said the old woman. "Oh! if I could only hear a priest say to me, 'Thy sins are forgiven!' I should believe it then."

The stranger turned towards her, and the goodness in his face made her tremble.

"Have faith," he said, "and you will be saved."

"May God reward you, good sir," she answered. "If what you say is true, I will go on pilgrimage barefooted to Our Lady of Loretto to pray to her for you and for me."

The two peasants, father and son, were silent, patient, and submissive to the will of God, like folk whose wont it is to fall in instinctively with the ways of Nature like cattle. At the one end of the boat stood riches, pride, learning, debauchery, and crime—human society, such as art and thought and education and worldly interests and laws have made it; and at this end there was terror and wailing, innumerable different impulses all repressed by hideous doubts—at this end, and at this only, the agony of fear.

Above all these human lives stood a strong man, the skipper; no doubts assailed him, the chief, the king, the fatalist among them. He was trusting in himself rather than in Providence, crying, "Bail away!" instead of "Holy Virgin," defying the storm, in fact, and struggling with the sea like a wrestler.

But the helpless poor at the other end of the wherry! The mother rocking on her bosom the little one who smiled at the storm; the woman once so frivolous and gay, and now tormented with bitter remorse; the old soldier covered with scars, a mutilated life the sole reward of his unflagging loyalty and faithfulness. This veteran could scarcely count on the morsel of bread soaked in tears to keep the life in him, yet he was always ready to laugh, and went his way merrily, happy when he could drown his glory in the depths of a pot of beer, or could tell tales of the wars to the children who admired him, leaving his future with a light heart in the hands of God. Lastly, there were the two peasants, used to hardships and toil, labor incarnate, the labor by which the world lives. These simple folk were indifferent to thought and its treasures, ready to sink them all in a belief; and their faith was but so much the more vigorous because they had never disputed about it nor analyzed it. Such a nature is a virgin soil, conscience has not been tampered with, feeling is deep and strong; repentance, trouble, love, and work have developed, purified, concentrated, and increased their force of will a hundred times, the will—the one thing in man that resembles what learned doctors call the Soul.

The boat, guided by the well-nigh miraculous skill of the steersman, came almost within sight of Ostend, when, not fifty paces from the shore, she was suddenly struck by a heavy sea and capsized. The stranger with the light about his head spoke to this little world of drowning creatures:

"Those who have faith shall be saved; let them follow me!"

He stood upright, and walked with a firm step upon the waves. The young mother at once took her child in her arms, and followed at his side across the sea. The soldier too sprang up, saying in his homely fashion, "Ah! *nom d'un pipe*! I would follow *you* to the devil;" and without seeming astonished by it, he walked on the water. The worn-out sinner, believing in the omnipotence of God, also followed the stranger.

The two peasants said to each other, "If they are walking on the sea, why should we not do as they do?" and they also arose and hastened after the others. Thomas tried to follow, but his faith tottered; he sank in the sea more than once, and rose again, but the third time he also walked on the sea. The bold steersman clung like a remora to the wreck of his boat. The miser had had faith, and had risen to go, but he tried to take his gold with him, and it was his gold that dragged him down to the bottom. The learned man had scoffed at the charlatan and at the fools who listened to him; and when he heard the mysterious stranger propose to the passengers that they should walk on the waves, he began to laugh, and the ocean swallowed him. The girl was dragged down into the depths by her lover. The Bishop and the older lady went to the bottom, heavily laden with sins, it may be, but still more heavily laden with incredulity and confidence in idols, weighted down by devotion, into which alms-deeds and true religion entered but little.

The faithful flock, who walked with a firm step high and dry above the surge, heard all about them the dreadful whistling of the blast; great billows broke across their path, but an irresistible force cleft a way for them through the sea. These believing ones saw through the spray a dim speck of light flickering in the window of a fisherman's hut on the shore, and each one, as he pushed on bravely towards the light, seemed to hear the voice of his fellow crying, "Courage!" through all the roaring of the surf; yet no one had spoken a word—so absorbed was each by his own peril. In this way they reached the shore.

When they were all seated near the fisherman's fire, they looked round in vain for their guide with the light about him. The sea washed up the steersman at the base of the cliff on which the cottage stood; he was clinging with might and main to the plank as a sailor can cling when death stares him in the face; the MAN went down and rescued the almost exhausted seaman; then he said, as he held out a succoring hand above the man's head:

"Good, for this once; but do not try it again; the example would be too bad."

He took the skipper on his shoulders, and carried him to the fisherman's door; knocked for admittance for the exhausted man; then, when the door of the humble refuge opened, the Saviour disappeared.

The Convent of Mercy was built for sailors on this spot, where for long afterwards (so it was said) the footprints of Jesus Christ could be seen in the sand; but in 1793, at the time of the French invasion, the monks carried away this precious relic, that bore witness to the Saviour's last visit to earth.

There at the convent I found myself shortly after the Revolution of 1830. I was weary of life. If you had asked me the reason of my despair, I should have found it almost impossible to give it, so languid had grown the soul that was melted within me. The west wind had slackened the springs of my intelligence. A cold gray light poured down from the heavens, and the murky clouds that passed overhead gave a boding look to the land; all these things, together with the immensity of the sea, said to me, "Die to-day or die to-morrow, still must we not die?" And then—I wandered on, musing on the doubtful future, on my blighted hopes. Gnawed by these gloomy thoughts, I turned mechanically into the convent church, with the gray towers that loomed like ghosts though the sea mists. I looked round with no kindling of the imagination at the forest of columns, at the slender arches set aloft upon the leafy capitals, a delicate labyrinth of sculpture. I walked with careless eyes along the side aisles that opened out before me like vast portals, ever turning upon their hinges. It was scarcely possible to see, by the dim light of the autumn day, the sculptured groinings of the roof, the delicate and clean-cut lines of the mouldings of the graceful pointed arches. The organ pipes were mute. There was no sound save the noise of my own footsteps to awaken the mournful echoes lurking in the dark chapels. I sat down at the base of one of the four pillars that supported the tower, near the choir. Thence I could see the whole of the building. I gazed, and no ideas connected with it arose in my mind. I saw without seeing the mighty maze of pillars, the great rose windows that hung like a network suspended as by a miracle in air above the vast doorways. I saw the doors at the end of the side aisles, the aerial galleries, the stained glass windows framed in archways, divided by slender columns, fretted into flower forms and trefoil by fine filigree work of carved stone. A dome of glass at the end of the choir sparkled as if it had been built of precious stones set cunningly. In contrast to the roof with its alternating spaces of whiteness and color, the two aisles lay to right and left in shadow so deep that the faint gray outlines of their hundred shafts were scarcely visible in the gloom. I gazed at the marvelous arcades, the scroll-work, the garlands, the curving lines, and arabesques interwoven and interlaced, and strangely lighted, until by sheer dint of gazing my perceptions became confused, and I stood upon the borderland between illusion and reality, taken in the snare set for the eyes, and almost light-headed by reason of the multitudinous changes of the shapes about me.

Imperceptibly a mist gathered about the carven stonework, and I only beheld it through a haze of fine golden dust, like the motes that hover in the bars of sunlight slanting through the air of a chamber. Suddenly the stone lacework of the rose windows gleamed through this vapor that had made all forms so shadowy. Every moulding, the edges of every carving, the least detail of the sculpture was dipped in silver. The sunlight kindled fires in the stained windows, their rich colors sent out glowing sparks of light. The shafts began to tremble, the capitals were gently shaken. A light shudder as of delight ran through the building, the stones were loosened in their setting, the wall-spaces swayed with graceful caution. Here and there a ponderous pier moved as solemnly as a dowager when she condescends to complete a quadrille at the close of a ball. A few slender and graceful columns, their heads adorned with wreaths of trefoil, began to laugh and dance here and there. Some of the pointed arches dashed at the tall lancet windows, who, like ladies of the Middle Ages, wore the armorial bearings of their houses emblazoned on their golden robes. The dance of the mitred arcades with the slender windows became like a fray at a tourney.

In another moment every stone in the church vibrated, without leaving its place; for the organ-pipes spoke, and I heard divine music mingling with the songs of angels, and unearthly harmony, accompanied by the deep notes of the bells, that boomed as the giant towers rocked and swayed on their square bases. This strange Sabbath seemed to me the most natural thing in the world; and I, who had seen Charles X. hurled from his throne, was no longer amazed by anything. Nay, I myself was gently swaying with a see-saw movement that influenced my nerves pleasurably in a manner of which it is impossible to give any idea. Yet in the midst of this heated riot, the cathedral choir felt cold as if it were a winter day, and I became aware of a multitude of women, robed in white, silent, and impassive, sitting there. The sweet incense smoke that arose from the censers was grateful to my soul. The tall wax candles flickered. The lectern, gay as a chanter undone by the treachery of wine, was skipping about like a peal of Chinese bells.

Then I knew that the whole cathedral was whirling round so fast that everything appeared to be undisturbed. The colossal Figure on the crucifix above the altar smiled upon me with a mingled malice and benevolence that frightened me; I turned my eyes away, and marveled at the bluish vapor that slid across the pillars, lending to them an indescribable charm. Then some graceful women's forms began to stir on the friezes. The cherubs who upheld the heavy columns shook out their wings. I felt myself uplifted by some divine power that steeped me in infinite joy, in a sweet and languid rapture. I would have given my life, I think, to have prolonged these phantasmagoria for a little, but suddenly a shrill voice clamored in my ears:

"Awake and follow me!"

A withered woman took my hand in hers; its icy coldness crept through every nerve. The bones of her face showed plainly through the sallow, almost olive-tinted wrinkles of the skin. The shrunken, ice-cold old woman wore a black robe, which she trailed in the dust, and at her throat there was something white, which I dared not examine. I could scarcely see her wan and colorless eyes, for they were fixed in a stare upon the heavens. She drew me after her along the aisles, leaving a trace of her presence in the ashes that she shook from her dress. Her bones rattled as she walked, like the bones of a skeleton; and as we went I heard behind me the tinkling of a little bell, a thin, sharp sound that rang through my head like the notes of a harmonica.

"Suffer!" she cried, "suffer! So it must be!"

We came out of the church; we went through the dirtiest streets of the town, till we came at last to a dingy dwelling, and she bade me enter in. She dragged me with her, calling to me in a harsh, tuneless voice like a cracked bell:

"Defend me! defend me!"

Together we went up a winding staircase. She knocked at a door in the darkness, and a mute, like some familiar of the Inquisition, opened to her. In another moment we stood in a room hung with ancient, ragged tapestry, amid piles of old linen, crumpled muslin, and gilded brass.

"Behold the wealth that shall endure for ever!" said she.

I shuddered with horror; for just then, by the light of a tall torch and two altar candles, I saw distinctly that this woman was fresh from the graveyard. She had no hair. I turned to fly. She raised her fleshless arm and encircled me with a band of iron set with spikes, and as she raised it a cry went up all about us, the cry of millions of voices—the shouting of the dead!

"It is my purpose to make thee happy for ever," she said. "Thou art my son."

We were sitting before the hearth, the ashes lay cold upon it; the old shrunken woman grasped my hand so tightly in hers that I could not choose but stay. I looked fixedly at her, striving to read the story of her life from the things among which she was crouching. Had she indeed any life in her? It was a mystery. Yet I saw plainly that once she must have been young and beautiful; fair, with all the charm of simplicity, perfect as some Greek statue, with the brow of a vestal.

"Ah! ah!" I cried, "now I know thee! Miserable woman, why hast thou prostituted thyself? In the age of thy passions, in the time of thy prosperity, the grace and purity of thy youth were forgotten. Forgetful of thy heroic devotion, thy pure life, thy abundant faith, thou didst resign thy primitive power and thy spiritual supremacy for fleshly power. Thy linen vestments, thy couch of moss, the cell in the rock, bright with rays of the Light Divine, was forsaken; thou hast sparkled with diamonds, and shone with the glitter of luxury and pride. Then, grown bold and insolent, seizing and overturning all things in thy course like a courtesan eager for pleasure in her days of splendor, thou hast steeped thyself in blood like some queen stupefied by empery.

Dost thou not remember to have been dull and heavy at times, and the sudden marvelous lucidity of other moments; as when Art emerges from an orgy? Oh! poet, painter, and singer, lover of splendid ceremonies and protector of the arts, was thy friendship for art perchance a caprice, that so thou shouldst sleep beneath magnificent canopies? Was there not a day when, in thy fantastic pride, though chastity and humility were prescribed to thee, thou hadst brought all things beneath thy feet, and set thy foot on the necks of princes; when earthly dominion, and wealth, and the mind of man bore thy yoke? Exulting in the abasement of humanity, joying to witness the uttermost lengths to which man's folly would go, thou hast bidden thy lovers walk on all fours, and required of them their lands and wealth, nay, even their wives if they were worth aught to thee. Thou hast devoured millions of men without a cause; thou hast flung away lives like sand blown by the wind from West to East. Thou hast come down from the heights of thought to sit among the kings of men. Woman! instead of comforting men, thou hast tormented and afflicted them! Knowing that thou couldst ask and have, thou hast demanded—blood! A little flour surely should have contented thee, accustomed as thou hast been to live on bread and to mingle water with thy wine. Unlike all others in all things, formerly thou wouldst bid thy lovers fast, and they obeyed. Why should thy fancies have led thee to require things impossible? Why, like a courtesan spoiled by her lovers, hast thou doted on follies, and left those undeceived who sought to explain and justify all thy errors? Then came the days of thy later passions, terrible like the love of a woman of forty years, with a fierce cry thou hast sought to clasp the whole universe in one last embrace—and thy universe recoiled from thee!

"Then old men succeeded to thy young lovers; decrepitude came to thy feet and made thee hideous. Yet, even then, men with the eagle power of vision said to thee in a glance, 'Thou shalt perish ingloriously, because thou hast fallen away, because thou hast broken the vows of thy maidenhood. The angel with peace written on her forehead, who should have shed light and joy along her path, has been a Messalina, delighting in the circus, in debauchery, and abuse of power. The days of thy virginity cannot return; henceforward thou shalt be subject to a master. Thy hour has come; the hand of death is upon thee. Thy heirs believe that thou art rich; they will kill thee and find nothing. Yet try at least to fling away this raiment no longer in fashion; be once more as in the days of old!—Nay, thou art dead, and by thy own deed!'

"Is not this thy story?" so I ended. "Decrepit, toothless, shivering crone, now forgotten, going thy ways without so much as a glance from passers-by! Why art thou still alive? What doest thou in that beggar's garb, uncomely and desired of none? Where are thy riches?—for what were they spent? Where are thy treasures?—what great deeds hast thou done?"

At this demand, the shriveled woman raised her bony form, flung off her rags, and grew tall and radiant, smiling as she broke forth from the dark chrysalid sheath. Then like a butterfly, this diaphanous creature emerged, fair and youthful, clothed in white linen, an Indian from creation issuing her palms. Her golden hair rippled over her shoulders, her eyes glowed, a bright mist clung about her, a ring of gold hovered above her head, she shook the flaming blade of a sword towards the spaces of heaven.

"See and believe!" she cried.

And suddenly I saw, afar off, many thousands of cathedrals like the one that I had just quitted; but these were covered with pictures and with frescoes, and I heard them echo with entrancing music. Myriads of human creatures flocked to these great buildings, swarming about them like ants on an ant-heap. Some were eager to rescue books from oblivion or to copy manuscripts, others were helping the poor, but nearly all were studying. Up above this countless multitude rose giant statues that they had erected in their midst, and by the gleams of a strange light from some luminary as powerful as the sun, I read the inscriptions on the bases of the statues—Science, History, Literature.

The light died out. Again I faced the young girl. Gradually she slipped into the dreary sheath, into the ragged cere-cloths, and became an aged woman again. Her familiar brought her a little dust, and she stirred it into the ashes of her chafing-dish, for the weather was cold and stormy; and then he lighted for her, whose palaces had been lit with thousands of wax-tapers, a little cresset, that she might see to read her prayers through the hours of night.

"There is no faith left in the earth!..." she said.

In such a perilous plight did I behold the fairest and the greatest, the truest and most life-giving of all Powers.

"Wake up, sir, the doors are just about to be shut," said a hoarse voice. I turned and beheld the beadle's ugly countenance; the man was shaking me by the arm, and the cathedral lay wrapped in shadows as a man is wrapped in his cloak.

"Belief," I said to myself, "is Life! I have just witnessed the funeral of a monarchy, now we must defend the church."

PARIS, February 1831.

www.ingramcontent.com/pod-product-compliance
Ingram Content Group UK Ltd.
Pitfield, Milton Keynes, MK11 3LW, UK
UKHW031340260325
456749UK00002B/274